Incarceration Issues:
Punishment, Reform, and Rehabilitation

TITLE LIST

PRISONERS ON DEATH ROW

by Roger Smith

Mason Crest Publishers
Philadelphia

Mason Crest Publishers Inc.
370 Reed Road
Broomall, Pennsylvania 19008
(866) MCP-BOOK (toll free)

First printing
1 2 3 4 5 6 7 8 9 10

Library of Congress Cataloging-in-Publication Data

Smith, Roger, 1959 Aug. 15–
  Prisoners on death row / by Roger Smith.
      p. cm. — (Incarceration issues)
  Includes index.
  ISBN 1-59084-989-2   ISBN 1-59084-984-1 (series)
  ISBN 978-1-59084-989-7   ISBN 978-1-59084-984-2 (series)

  1. Death row. 2. Death row inmates. I. Title. II. Series.
  HV8694.S64 2006
  364.66092'273—dc22
                         2005029518

Interior design by MK Bassett-Harvey.
Interiors produced by Harding House Publishing Service, Inc.
www.hardinghousepages.com

Cover design by Peter Spires Culotta.

Printed in India by Quadra Press.

Contents

INTRODUCTION

by Larry E. Sullivan, Ph.D.

Prisons will be with us as long as we have social enemies. We will punish them for acts that we consider criminal, and we will confine them in institutions.

Prisons have a long history, one that fits very nicely in the religious context of sin, evil, guilt, and expiation. In fact, the motto of one of the first prison reform organizations was "Sin no more." Placing offenders in prison was, for most of the history of the prison, a ritual for redemption through incarceration; hence the language of punishment takes on a very theological cast. The word "penitentiary" itself comes from the religious concept of penance. When we discuss prisons, we are dealing not only with the law but with very strong emotions and reactions to acts that range from minor or misdemeanor crimes to major felonies like murder and rape.

Prisons also reflect the level of the civilizing process through which a culture travels, and it tells us much about how we treat our fellow human beings. The great nineteenth-century Russian author Fyodor Dostoyevsky, who was a political prisoner, remarked, "The degree of civilization in a society can be measured by observing its prisoners." Similarly, Winston Churchill, the great British prime minister during World War II, said that the "treatment of crime and criminals is one of the most unfailing tests of civilization of any country."

Since the very beginnings of the American Republic, we have attempted to improve and reform the way we imprison criminals. For much of the history of the American prison, we tried to rehabilitate or modify the criminal behavior of offenders through a variety of treatment programs. In the last quarter of the twentieth century, politicians and citizens alike realized that this attempt had failed, and we began passing stricter laws, imprisoning people for longer terms and building more prisons. This movement has taken a great toll on society. Approximately two million people are behind bars today. This movement has led to the

overcrowding of prisons, worse living conditions, fewer educational programs, and severe budgetary problems. There is also a significant social cost, since imprisonment splits families and contributes to a cycle of crime, violence, drug addiction, and poverty.

All these are reasons why this series on incarceration issues is extremely important for understanding the history and culture of the United States. Readers will learn all facets of punishment: its history; the attempts to rehabilitate offenders; the increasing number of women and juveniles in prison; the inequality of sentencing among the races; attempts to find alternatives to incarceration; the high cost, both economically and morally, of imprisonment; and other equally important issues. These books teach us the importance of understanding that the prison system affects more people in the United States than any institution, other than our schools.

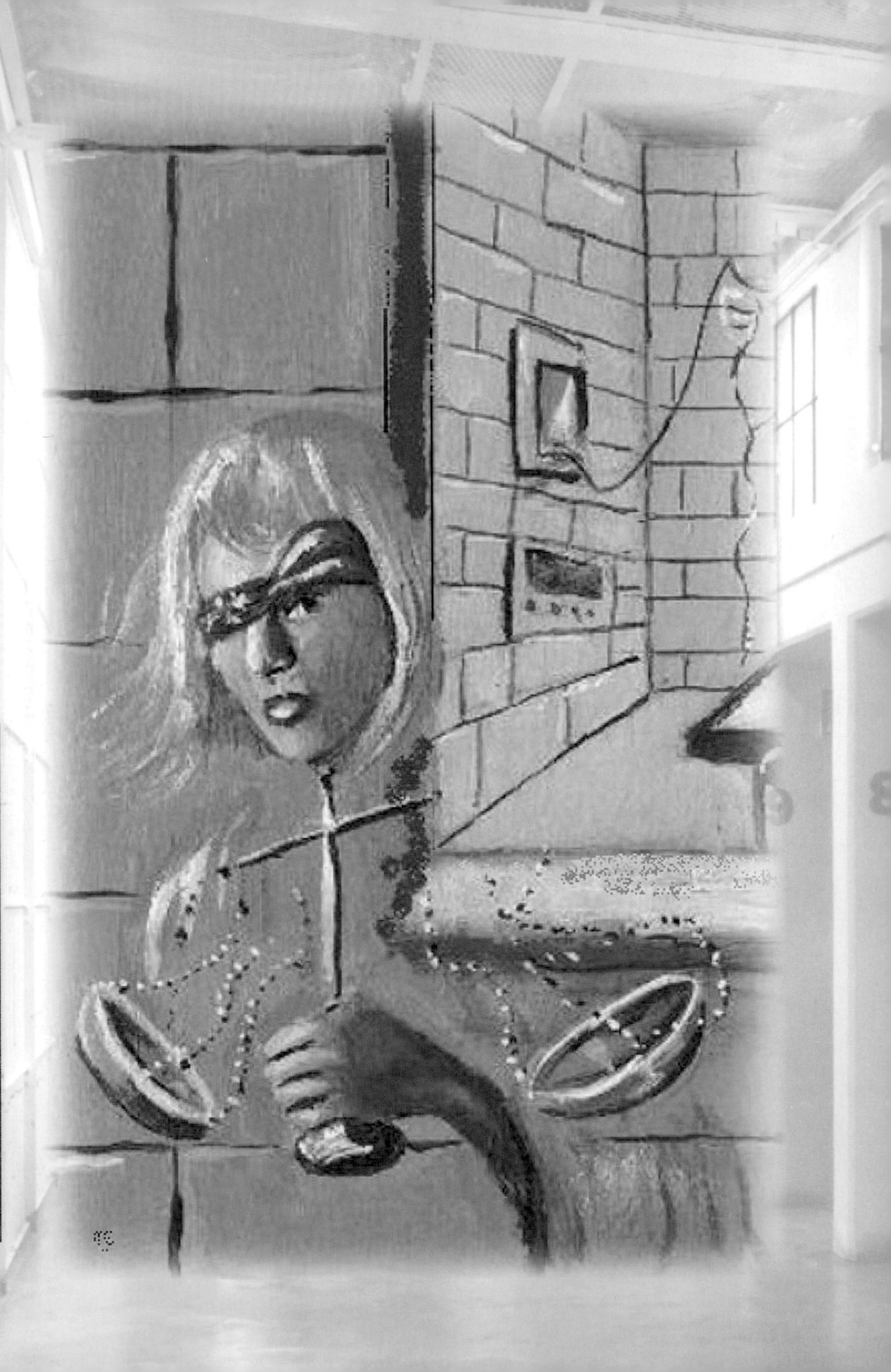

CHAPTER 1.

LIFE FOR LIFE: THE ULTIMATE SOCIAL CONTROVERSY

On March 15, 2000, a twenty-year saga of murder, trials, and appeals ended when state corrections officials executed Patrick Poland by lethal injection in Florence, Arizona. He was the twenty-fourth death row inmate put to death in the United States that year; it was the 621st since the reinstatement of the U.S. death penalty in 1976.

The crime behind the case happened twenty-three years before. On May 24, 1977, two guards, Russell Dempsey and Cecil Newkirk, left Phoenix, Arizona, in an armored van on their route to banks in the northern part of the state. At the

How should violence be punished?

Bumblebee Road exit on Interstate 17, Michael and Patrick Poland stopped them. Disguised as highway patrol officers, the brothers were driving a car modified to look like a police car. Later investigation showed that the Polands had spent weeks carefully planning this deception. The brothers captured the guards and stole nearly $300,000 in cash.

Three days later, authorities found the abandoned armored van. The same day, Michael Poland rented a boat at the Lake Mead marina and piloted the craft to a remote dock, where he met Patrick. The two brothers stuffed the guards into specially made canvas bags and dumped them into the lake. Three weeks later, the decomposing bodies of Dempsey and Newkirk surfaced, while the Poland brothers were spending money freely.

Two months later, the FBI got a search warrant for Michael Poland's home, where they found items he had used to impersonate a police officer. They also attained a warrant for Patrick's house, where they found more evidence. So, on May 17, 1978, the federal government charged Patrick and Michael Poland with five counts of bank robbery, two counts

Impersonating a police officer is a crime—but the Poland brothers had far worse offenses on their rap sheets.

The Poland brothers were convicted in federal court of robbery and kidnapping, while the state court found them guilty of murder.

of kidnapping, and two counts of murder. The government offered the brothers a **plea bargain**, which they refused. The brothers were convicted in federal court on robbery and kidnapping charges, and in state court on murder charges. The Polands claimed that one guard had died of a heart attack after his capture, and this had forced them to kill the second guard. This argument did nothing to sway the courts.

For the next twenty years, there was a series of appeals, but by 1999, these were exhausted. Awaiting execution, Michael Poland unsuccessfully attempted to escape from prison. He was executed first, on June 16, 1999. For his last meal (as recorded by the Arizona Department of Corrections), he ordered three fried eggs, sunny side up; four slices of bacon; an order of hash browns; two slices of whole wheat toast, with two pats of real butter; two individual-serving boxes of Raisin Bran cereal; two cartons of milk; and two cups of Tasters Choice coffee. Despite that, his last

A lethal injection table looks a little like a hospital gurney.

words were, "I'd like to know if you're going to bring me lunch afterward; I'm really hungry. I can't think of anything else."

A year later, Patrick followed his brother's steps to the death chamber, but the younger brother's execution was more controversial: there was a last-minute appeal to save his life. Melvin McDonald, the prosecutor who put the Poland brothers on death row, tried to save Patrick Poland from execution. He agreed with the arguments of Patrick Poland's family members: Poland's brothers and sister told of the abuse he had suffered as a child and how he fell under the influence of his older brother, Michael. They said the "evil" older brother led Patrick into crime and murder. Patrick Poland's daughter, Stacey, said if she could start her life over and pick any father, she would still choose Patrick Poland. However, the victims' families also had their say: in light of their suffering, Poland's death was justified.

The morning of his execution, Patrick Poland requested no special meal. He spent his last hours with a priest, confessing his sins and asking forgiveness, and then he was strapped to a **gurney** and wheeled into the execution chamber. Minutes before death, he apologized to the families of his victims: "I'm sincere. I'm sorry for the pain and suffering I have caused. I do thank you for your forgiveness." He also spoke to his girlfriend, Sherri Jo Christensen, who attended the execution, assuring her of his love. At 3:03 P.M., the executioner injected lethal chemicals into Patrick Poland; four minutes later, he was dead. According to an Associated Press release, "Yavapai County prosecutor Arthur Markham, who did not prosecute the case, spoke to some of the victims' relatives afterward and said they felt his expressions of remorse were truthful. 'A man would not lie just before death,' Markham said."

While every death penalty case is unique, the Poland case typifies the ways that the death penalty divides Americans. For the families of the Patrick Poland's victims, it was a long-awaited and just outcome for the brutal death of their loved ones; but for the friends and family of Patrick Poland, it was a sad and unnecessary death. The death penalty is an emotional, complex, and vital issue for criminals, courts, victims, advocates, justice officers, and ordinary citizens in the United States today.

DEATH PENALTY HISTORY

For thousands of years, societies used the death penalty as punishment for murder and other crimes. One of the most ancient law codes, the Babylonian Code of Hammurabi, lists death as the punishment for the following offenses: giving false testimony; making unproved accusations; theft from temples, state property, or the household of a landowner; receiving stolen goods; helping slaves escape or hiding runaway slaves; damaging the wall of a house; robbery; failure to heed the summons of the king; cheating in the selling of wine; allowing outlaws to congregate in a house without reporting them; violating vows; humiliating a husband; or poor house construction that caused a death.

Crucifixion was a common form of execution used during the time of the Roman Empire.

The Bible is another ancient document that includes the death penalty. Jewish and Christian children are familiar with the story of Noah's ark, but the children's version usually does not include God's words to Noah after the ark landed: "Whoever sheds the blood of man, by man shall his blood be shed" (Genesis 9:6). Likewise, Moses commanded the ancient Jews that murder should be punished, "life for life" (Exodus 21:23). The common form of execution in ancient Israel was stoning, performed by an entire village. Ancient Egyptians and Greeks also punished a number of crimes by death.

This French guillotine was last used in 1960.

For thousands of years, Western civilization relied on death as punishment. Executions were public events, made gory in order to warn others against committing crimes. While ancient Rome was technologically an advanced civilization, it was also brutal in its treatment of wrongdoers: they threw criminals from cliffs, tortured them to death, fed them to wild animals, killed them by gladiators, and crucified them. The Middle Ages were no less ***barbarous***: officials executed criminals by public drowning, pulling their bodies apart, poking them with burning irons, and burning them alive. Executions continued to be common into the colonial era of Western history. Public hangings were common in England and the American colonies into the 1800s, and the ***guillotine*** was infamous for thousands of beheadings during the French revolution.

TWENTIETH-CENTURY OPINIONS

The late 1900s saw a dramatic shift in world opinion as government executions fell out of favor. In 1948, the United Nations (UN) adopted the Universal Declaration of Human Rights in 1948, which proclaimed a universal "right to life." Knowing that worldwide abolition of the death penalty would take decades to achieve, the UN focused on limiting the death penalty to protect children, pregnant women, and elderly prisoners from execution. During the 1950s and 1960s, nations drafted a number of international human rights treaties, including the International Covenant on Civil and Political Rights, the European Convention on Human Rights, and the American Convention on Human Rights. These documents limited but did not eliminate the death penalty.

In the closing decades of the twentieth century, an increasing number of national governments agreed with Amnesty International: "The death penalty is the ultimate cruel, inhuman and degrading punishment." Furthermore, thinkers around the world increasingly agreed with the UN that the right to life was a basic human right. In 1976, Portugal outlawed capital punishment; in 1978, Denmark followed their lead, and in 1979

Hangings were once a common form of American execution. Today, the United States is one of the few developed nations that continues to support the death penalty.

Luxembourg, Nicaragua, and Norway followed suit. In the following decades, hardly a year went by without several nations banning the practice.

THE WORLD TODAY

As of mid-2005, 120 nations have done away with government executions either by law or in actual practice. Only seventy-six countries retain the use of *capital punishment*. The European Union (EU), representing twenty-five member nations, has stated its opposition to the death penalty "in all cases" and committed itself to worldwide abolition of the penalty. Furthermore, countries cannot become members of the EU unless they agree to eliminate capital punishment. UN secretary general Kofi Annan has also endorsed a request that all nations of the world halt public executions. Nine out of eleven former Soviet states have abolished the death penalty (Belarus and Uzbekistan are exceptions).

THE UNITED STATES GOES AGAINST THE TREND

Due to its size and influence, the United States holds a unique role in its continuing support of the death penalty. In 2003, China, Iran, the United States, and Vietnam topped the world in executions. The northern and southern neighbors of the United States (Mexico and Canada) have both abolished the death penalty, as have a number of other nations in the Americas. While more than seventy nations continue executing criminals, the United States differs in a number of respects from other death penalty nations. The United States and Japan, out of the remaining death penalty nations, are "developed" nations (wealthy and *industrialized*)—as opposed to "Third World" (developing) countries—and the Japanese use the death penalty only very rarely. The United States is thus the only

Execution by firing squad was a common form of execution in the military. It was also used in Utah in 1977 for a civilian.

economically developed and democratic nation that continues significant use of the death penalty.

This exceptional support of the death penalty has cost the United States in terms of its reputation among other nations. The official EU Web site says, "The EU is deeply concerned about the increasing number of executions in the United States of America." The American Bar Association (ABA) Web site notes, "Without doubt, death penalty practices in the United States have damaged its international standing."

THE DEATH PENALTY IN THE UNITED STATES

While European nations were abandoning capital punishment in the last years of the twentieth century, the United States considered a series of cases relating to the death penalty, which eventually resulted in continuing executions.

In 1972, the United States Supreme Court cases of *Furman v. Georgia*, *Jackson v. Georgia*, and *Branch v. Texas* determined that a punishment would be "cruel and unusual" if it was too severe for the crime committed, if it was **arbitrary**, if it offended society's sense of justice, or it if was not more effective than a less severe penalty would be. As a result, the Supreme Court declared forty death penalty laws to be invalid, thereby overturning the sentences of 629 death row inmates around the country and suspending the death penalty. It is important to note that the Court did not deem the death penalty itself to be unconstitutional; they merely stated that the way it was used violated the Constitution. Thus, while executions were halted, they were not abolished.

Death row in San Quentin Prison

Shortly after the Furman case, the states of Florida, Georgia, and Texas set to work rewriting their laws concerning sentencing procedures for the death penalty in order to reinstate that form of punishment. In 1976, the Supreme Court ruled in *Gregg v. Georgia*, *Jurek v. Texas*, and *Proffitt v. Florida*, collectively known as the *Gregg* decision, that the new death penalty statutes in Florida, Georgia, and Texas were constitutional and that the death penalty itself was constitutional under the Eighth Amendment. Executions in the United States resumed on January 17, 1977, with the execution by firing squad of Gary Gilmore in Utah.

Currently, thirty-seven states and the federal government have the death penalty. No one in the United States has been executed for a crime other than murder or conspiracy to commit murder since 1964, and all death row inmates in 2002 had been convicted of murder. Since 1976,

Does taking a murderer's life balance the scales of justice?

972 convicted murderers have been executed in the United States. As of 2005, almost all states and the federal government have adopted lethal injection as the mode of execution. Also as of 2005, the United States is second only to China in passing death sentences.

JUSTIFICATIONS FOR THE ULTIMATE PENALTY

One argument for the death penalty is the concept of justice—the need to fulfill a philosophical or religious sense of "what is right." According to some **ethicists**, society should balance any crime with a punishment that is equal. For example, if a thief takes property, he should pay back the victim an equivalent amount. What then is the appropriate price to pay for taking a human life? According to David Anderson, author of *The Death Penalty—A Defence*, "Violent crimes and murder are part of the cruelest, most inhuman and disparaging crimes that exist and they violate the victim's right to life. . . . A lost human life can only be fully compensated through the death penalty."

In a recent article, *Fox News* contributor Tammy Bruce points to Manson family member Leslie Van Houten, convicted in 1969 for the murders of Leno LaBianca, a wealthy grocery store owner, and his wife, Rosemary; Van Houten stabbed Rosemary fifteen times. Bruce then notes the unfairness of Van Houten's possible release on parole. Is it just that members of the LaBianca family should forever suffer the loss of their loved ones, when Van Houten might again enjoy a free life? Bruce therefore states, "The death penalty is indeed a decent thing. Answering the monstrosity of the evil among us is our duty as decent people, as justice demands removing those who slaughter the innocent."

In 1997, a number of witnesses at the Timothy McVeigh trial described how the bomb set by McVeigh impacted their lives. Some expressed their belief that given their loss, the death penalty for McVeigh was necessary justice. "The sooner [McVeigh] meets his maker, the sooner justice will be served," said a woman whose four-year-old niece died in the blast.

These victims voiced a concern often used to explain why the death penalty should continue: **closure** for families of the victims. Closure is the right of victims to gain peace of mind through the death of a loved one's killer.

Supporters of the death penalty argue that capital punishment does more than right the wrongs of the past—it also works as **deterrence**, preventing future crimes. A study published in 2005 by two University of Chicago law professors found, "Recent evidence suggests that capital punishment may have a significant deterrent effect, preventing as many as eighteen or more murders for each execution."

CHALLENGING THE DEATH PENALTY'S EFFECTIVENESS

Those seeking to abolish capital punishment challenge all the reasons given for its use. Does the death penalty achieve justice? Cleveland judge

The Jewish scriptures allow for the death penalty—and yet "Thou shalt not kill" is also one of the Ten Commandments.

RELIGION AND THE DEATH PENALTY

In the beginning of the twenty-first century, religion continues to shape the lives and values of millions of people in the United States. Therefore, it is not surprising that religious beliefs and values influence opinions on the death penalty. The Jewish Bible (the Christian Old Testament), and the Muslim Koran all allow the use of the death penalty in certain cases. The Reverend Joe Ingle, a chaplain on death row in Nashville, Tennessee, says, "I don't think it's any accident. The Bible belt is also the death belt" (referring to the widespread support of capital punishment in the southern United States). However, numerous U.S. religious groups oppose the death penalty. Muhammad Sahli, former head of Richmond's Islamic Center of Virginia, opposes the death penalty because the Koran says God favors forgiveness for wrongdoers. Likewise, leaders of the Catholic Church base their opposition to the death penalty on their belief in the sanctity of life. Roger Mahoney, Catholic archbishop of Los Angeles, represents this Catholic position when he says, "Simply put, we believe that every person is sacred, every life is precious—even the life of one who has violated the rights of others by taking a life."

Daniel Gaul argues it does not: "Why do we kill people who kill people to prove that it's wrong to kill people?" Likewise, Rudolph Gerber, judge of the Arizona State Court of Appeals, says, "To support the death penalty . . . strikes me as grossly misguided. Not only does the death penalty not deter murder, it fosters a culture of brutality, risks international condemnation, and transforms our country into a brutal *pariah*." To its opponents, the death penalty is a violation of justice.

The question of closure is also the subject of vigorous debate, and some of those who suffered loss of a loved one by murder argue that the death of the killer will *not* bring them closure. Ronald W. Carlson, whose sister Deborah was murdered by Karla Faye Tucker in 1983, said:

> For eight years I wrestled with the death penalty issue in my life. I spent many hours and days pondering this way of life and death. I had hoped that maybe even witnessing the execution would have given me the closure that everyone speaks of. I have found that the death penalty did not solve any of that; however, I also have found that it does create more victims.

Religious leaders also have questioned the reality of closure for the families of victims. Roman Catholic Cardinal Anthony Bevilacqua told the *Philadelphia Inquirer* in 2000, "Closure and healing begin not with the taking of the offender's life as vengeance, but with forgiveness, which leads to true peace."

Opponents also challenge the death penalty's effectiveness as a deterrent. Some of the world's leading thinkers on matters of crime and punishment argue that it does no more to prevent crime than do other punishments. Former U.S. Supreme Court Justice Lewis Powell said, "It does not deter murders. It serves no purpose." Backing such claims, opponents of the death penalty point out that the United States has higher murder rates than those nations that have ended state executions. If the death penalty prevented murders, the opposite would be expected.

UNFAIR USE OF THE DEATH PENALTY?

Opponents of capital punishment point not only to its ineffectiveness: they also claim the death penalty is unfairly used. One of the most serious complaints concerns issues of race and class. Opponents point to numerous studies showing that courts use the death penalty ***discriminately***. Amnesty International USA points out, "Since 1977, the overwhelming majority of death row defendants (over 80 percent) have been executed for killing white victims, although African-Americans make up about half of all crime victims."

Some prominent politicians, judges, and lawyers have claimed the death penalty is used unfairly, citing the difference money makes in avoiding execution. Frank Murphy, former governor of Michigan and former U.S. Supreme Court Justice, said, "It's always the poor man who has no money or power who pays with his life, while another criminal may have committed an identical crime, but who is wealthy and powerful and escapes the chair or noose." Former Supreme Court Justice William O. Douglas concurs: "One searches in vain for the execution of any member of the affluent strata of society." There is a bitter joke told by death row prisoners: "It's called capital punishment because if you have capital, you don't get the punishment."

Although slavery was abolished after the Civil War, race continues to play a role in American society. Most death row defendants are African Americans convicted of killing white victims—even though about half of all murder victims are black.

Some judges have spoken out against the death penalty, saying that its use is influenced by racial and economic discrimination.

Finally, opponents of the death penalty say that the death penalty has at times been used to execute innocent people, and there is no way for society to return the life of a person unfairly executed. Harry Fogle, former Chief Judge of the Sixth Judicial Circuit, Florida, said, "In my own experience, I know of four persons convicted of first-degree murder and sentenced to death, who were later found to be innocent." Former U.S. Supreme Court Judge Sandra Day O'Connor likewise stated, "If statistics are any indication, the system may well be allowing some innocent defendants to be executed. More often than we want to recognize, some innocent defendants have been convicted and sentenced to death."

APPEALS AND DELAYS

Most death row inmates in the United States wait more than a decade for execution, and some prisoners have been on death row for well over twenty years. Since the reinstatement of the death penalty in 1976, the Supreme Court has introduced numerous reforms to create a fairer system, and these have resulted in a lengthy cycle of appeals and retrials.

Because of the number of delays, appeals, and retrials, the average death penalty case in America costs over a million dollars. By contrast, the average life-sentence case costs half that amount. The delay caused has also led to the graying of the death row population: 110 prisoners were at least 60 years old as of 2003.

The length of time prisoners spend on death row awaiting execution has raised some difficult issues. Is the state sentencing death row inmates to a double punishment—a long and unpleasant imprisonment in harsh conditions in addition to their death? A case argued before the European Court of Human Rights claimed that conditions a convict faces during the lengthy period between sentencing and execution are as psychologically damaging as torture. Despite the controversy over the number of appeals death row inmates are allowed, one thing on which death penalty supporters and critics agree is that it is vitally important not to make mistakes regarding executions. The long *appellate* process helps avoid irreversible errors.

Capital punishment is one of the most divisive and emotional debates in the United States today. Both sides claim they are literally fighting for life—either the life of the condemned criminal or the lives of potential victims—and both sides claim to be upholding practices essential for a healthy society. In this chapter, we have discussed some of the theories about capital punishment, both pro and con: but death row is not about theories; it is about people's lives, both the lives of those awaiting execution and the lives of their victims.

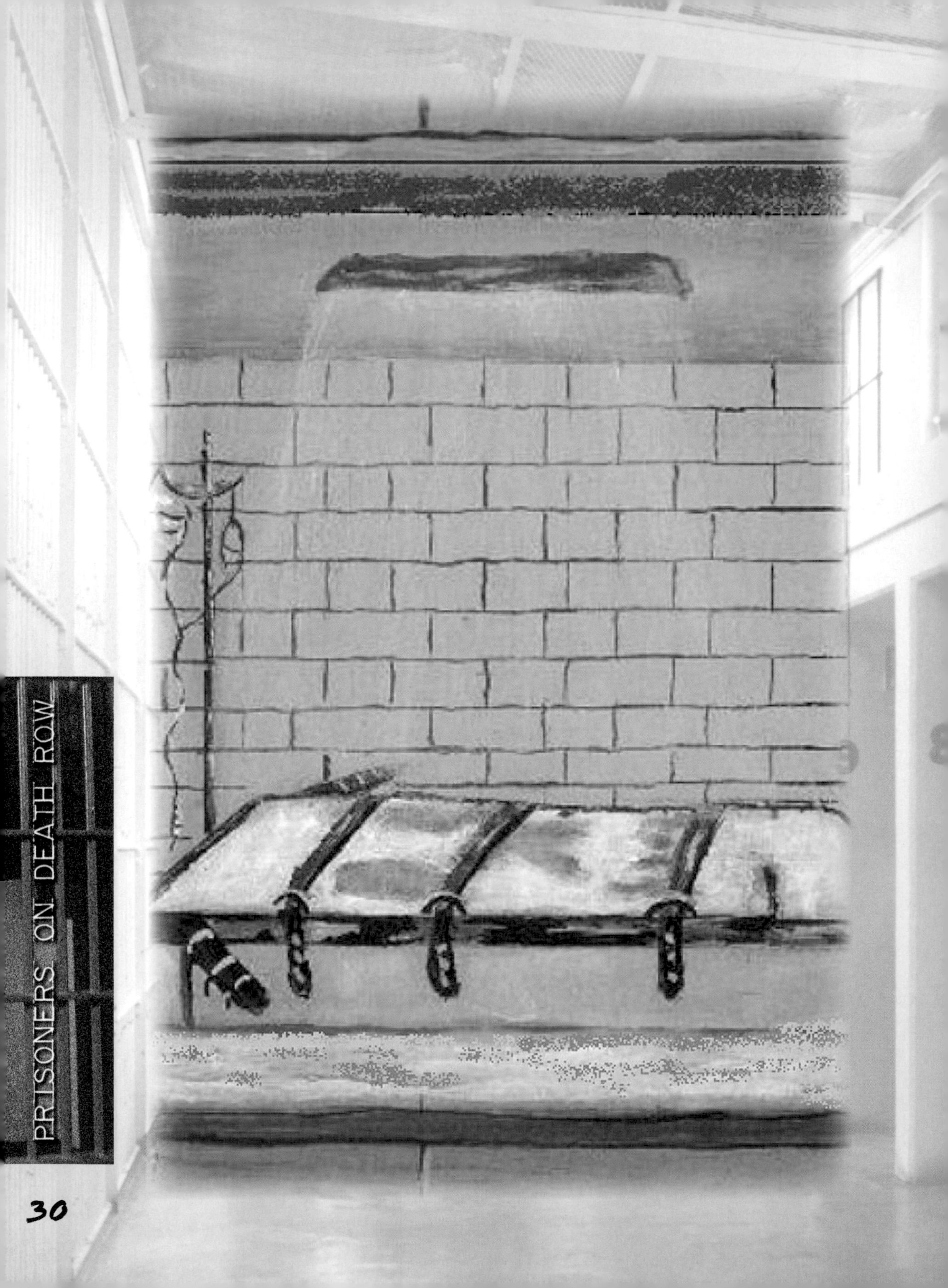

CHAPTER 2

DEATH ROW CASES

April 19, 1995, began as a typical sun-drenched morning in Oklahoma City; however, what seemed an ordinary day was about to explode into tragic chaos. At exactly 9:02 A.M., 4,000 pounds of explosives shattered the Alfred P. Murrah Federal Building into pieces. The blast was deafening, the force of it was so strong that a third of the building disappeared into a tangled jigsaw puzzle of glass, metal, and the bodies of men, women, and children. The bombing produced some examples of heroism: people risked their lives to help others escape the inferno, and there were tales of survivors pulled amazingly

out of the rubble. Nonetheless, the bombing was an unprecedented tragedy for Oklahoma City and for America: 168 people died, more than 500 were wounded, and countless hopes and dreams ended in the fiery blast. Just as the building became an inferno, the perpetrator, twenty-seven-year-old Timothy McVeigh, was driving away from the scene, wearing earplugs to protect himself from the deafening explosion.

McVeigh had served with the army in the Gulf War. He was skilled with all kinds of weapons and the military said he was a "good soldier." After the war, McVeigh became disillusioned with civilian life; it seemed no one wanted to employ a veteran, and he became convinced that the government and the army were part of a *liberal* conspiracy to destroy America. He was a supporter of David Koresh, the religious leader who armed his followers, the Branch Davidians, in Waco, Texas, to fight against federal agents. When the Branch Davidians' compound went up in flames on April 19, 1993, McVeigh committed himself to avenge the death of people he saw as patriots. McVeigh thought of himself as a patriot, as well, a soldier fighting for a better America. One of his favorite books was *The Turner Diaries*, in which hero Earl Turner responds to gun control by making a truck bomb and blowing up the Washington FBI Building.

Events after the Oklahoma City bombing quickly landed McVeigh in jail. Crime-scene investigators found pieces of the Ryder truck he had stuffed with explosives and detonated under the building, and they traced the truck's rental to McVeigh. In the meantime, a police officer had stopped McVeigh for driving without a proper license and for possessing a firearm. He was already in jail when authorities began searching for him in connection with the bombing.

McVeigh's accomplice, Terry Nichols, was arrested later.

On May 24, 1977, the trial of Timothy McVeigh began. The bomber's defense attorney was Stephen Jones. Though Jones had worked on behalf of many unpopular figures, he had never before attempted to defend someone who had killed 168 people. The prosecutor, Joseph Hartzler, presented an overwhelming amount of physical evidence connecting McVeigh to the bombing. Although Jones tried valiantly to throw suspicion onto an unidentified third man, the jury unanimously found that Timothy McVeigh deserved to die, and the judge told the jurors in the case, "You've done your job and done it well."

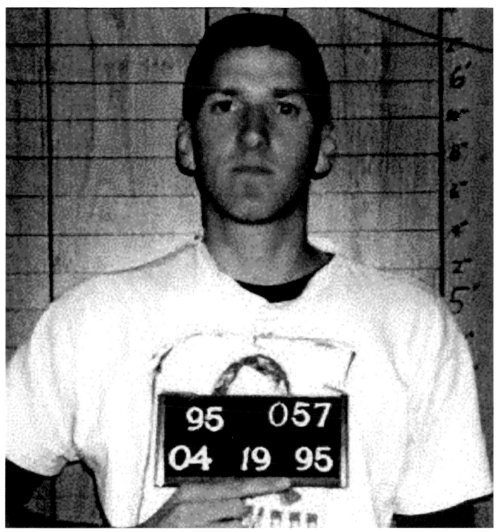

Timothy McVeigh's mug shot

McVeigh spent his last days at a "supermax" prison facility, where other notorious murderers resided. He was **unrepentant** to the end; he stated that the loss of life from the bombing was "unfortunate" but defended his actions as necessary in a war against an unjust government. On June 11, 2001, at 8:14 A.M., Timothy McVeigh died after prison authorities injected him with a lethal drug cocktail of sodium thiopental, pancuronium bromide, and potassium chloride. The execution, which took place at a federal prison in Terre Haute, Indiana, was broadcast to

The building across the street from the federal building in Oklahoma City was also damaged in the blast from McVeigh's bomb.

Oklahoma City, where 232 survivors and victims' relatives watched the execution. As his last statement, the defiant bomber left the poem "Invictus," written by William Ernst Henley:

Out of the night that covers me,
Black as the Pit from pole to pole,
I thank whatever gods may be
For my unconquerable soul.
In the fell clutch of circumstance
I have not winced nor cried aloud.
Under the bludgeonings of chance
My head is bloody, but unbowed.
Beyond this place of wrath and tears
Looms but the Horror of the shade,
And yet the menace of the years
Finds, and shall find, me unafraid.

The Oklahoma City bombing, where Timothy McVeigh was responsible for the deaths of 168 people.

Terry Nichols received a life sentence without parole for his part in the Oklahoma City bombing.

Recovery workers work on what was once a children's day-care center. That McVeigh seemed indifferent to the fact that children were inside the building he bombed convinced people he was a "monster" who deserved to die.

> It matters not how strait the gate,
> How charged with punishments the scroll,
> I am the master of my fate:
> I am the captain of my soul.

For many citizens, Timothy McVeigh's case was a prime example of the continuing need for the death penalty. McVeigh had very deliberately caused the death of 168 people, and wounded many more. Worst of all, he showed no regret for his actions; until death he was proud of his "patriotic war" against the government. For victims and others, McVeigh seemed less than human; he was a monster, and execution seemed to be a fully justified outcome for such a creature. Terry Nichols received a sentence of life without parole for his part in the bombings, as a Texas jury was unable to agree on the death penalty for Nichols.

Karla Faye Tucker

KARLA FAYE TUCKER: THE KILLER WHO CLAIMED TO BE REBORN

On June 13, 1983, Jerry Dean and Deborah Thornton were brutally murdered. The assailants were Karla Faye Tucker, a friend of Dean's estranged wife, Shawn, and Tucker's boyfriend, Danny Garrett. The couple, along

Tucker with Sr. Helen Prejean, who spoke out against the death penalty in her book *Dead Man Walking.*

with James Leibrant, had come to steal Dean's motorcycle. Armed with a pick axe and hammer, Tucker and Garrett beat and hacked at Dean and Thornton, leaving their mutilated bodies in piles of blood. Later, Tucker bragged that she got "a thrill" committing the vicious murder.

Danny Garrett's brother, Doug Garrett, told the police what his brother and Tucker had done, and the couple, along with Leibrant, was ultimately arrested. Leibrant, who had stayed outside during the violence, thinking it was only a robbery was freed. Garrett and Tucker were tried separately. During Tucker's trial, the jury heard details of the grisly killing and listened to a tape recording in which Tucker boasted of the murders. The trial juries found both Tucker and Garrett guilty, and they

An execution chamber for lethal injection

were sentenced to death for their crimes. Danny Garrett later died of liver disease while on death row awaiting execution.

Karla Faye Tucker had a rough life before she committed the brutal crime—a life filled with all sorts of bad choices. Her parents did little to guide her. She dropped out of school in seventh grade and became addicted to heroin shortly after. Tucker would claim that her mother turned her on to prostitution at age fourteen. Her teen years and young adulthood were a blur of addiction and sex.

According to her own story, Tucker experienced a religious conversion on death row. Seeking diversion from time spent in her cell, she attended a religious service, which made a profound impression. Returning to her quarters, she prayed with emotion, asking God to forgive her. Consequently, Tucker claimed to be "born again" spiritually. Eventually, she met, fell in love with, and married a minister who came to offer support to death row inmates. They were never allowed to spend time alone together; their marriage consisted of conversation through a screen that prevented physical contact.

The State of Texas executed Karla Faye Tucker by lethal injection on February 3, 1998, in one of the most controversial executions in U.S. history. During the days prior to the execution, there were several emotional appeals made to **commute** her sentence to a lengthy imprisonment. Several factors made Tucker's case unique. First, there was the gender issue; Texas had not executed any woman since the 1860s. Tucker's personality also made a difference; she was winsome, soft-spoken, and eloquent, and she made a good impression when interviewed live by Larry King three weeks before her execution.

Most important, Tucker claimed to be an entirely different person from the woman who murdered Jerry Dean and Deborah Thornton. According to Tucker, her Christian conversion had given her a new perspective on life. Charley Davidson, the prosecutor of Danny Garrett, stated in January 1998:

> The Karla Tucker who killed Jerry Dean and Debra Thornton cannot be executed by the State of Texas because that person no longer exists. The Karla Tucker who remains on death row is a

completely different person who, in my opinion, is not capable of those atrocities. . . . She is no longer a threat to society.

Tucker's case generated enormous public sympathy. On the day of the execution, the governor's office received 12,519 calls about the case; these calls were 4-to-1 against the execution. One significant aspect of the case was the way it changed *evangelical* Christians' opinions about the death penalty. Prior to the Karla Faye Tucker case, evangelicals generally supported the death penalty due to Bible verses permitting the practice. However, Tucker impressed conservative Christian leaders with her profession of faith. Pat Robertson, a well-known representative for evangelical Christianity, and *Christianity Today*, the leading evangelical magazine, both went on record opposing her execution. Tucker herself espoused a "consistent pro-life" position, opposing abortion, *euthanasia*, and the death penalty, based on the Christian belief in sanctity of life.

In the end, the Tucker execution rested in the hands of the Texas Board of Pardons and Paroles, which declined to commute her sentence. All Texas governor (and later U.S. president) George W. Bush could do was grant a thirty-day stay, which he refused, saying, "It's tough stuff, but my job is to enforce the law." Enforce it he did, leading to Tucker's execution.

Moments before her death, Tucker addressed those in attendance at her execution:

I would like to say to all of you, the Thornton family and Jerry Dean's family that I am so sorry. I hope God will give you peace with this. Baby, I love you. Ron, give Peggy a hug for me. Everybody has been so good to me. I love all of you very much. I'm going to be face to face with Jesus now. Warden Zaggett, thank all of you so much. You have been so good to me. I love all of you very much. I will see you all when you get there. I will wait for you.

Some of those who watched her execution were unimpressed by Tucker's claims to be a new person. Richard Thornton, the husband of

RACE AND THE DEATH PENALTY

The death sentence against Mumia Abu-Jamal has come to represent a larger issue: the gap between treatment of whites and blacks in death penalty sentencing. Supreme Court Justice Harry Blackmun wrote in 1994, "Even under the most sophisticated death penalty statutes, race continues to play a major role in determining who shall live and who shall die." Blacks in the United States are more likely to receive the death penalty than are whites; black males make up over 42 percent of all death row prisoners, though they account for only 6 percent of the U.S. population.

victim Deborah Thornton, said, "Justice for Deborah . . . is complete. . . . Fourteen and a half years ago, Karla Faye Tucker exploded my family . . . I don't believe her Christianity; I don't believe her conversion. I never did; I never will." However, Ronald Carlson, Deborah Thornton's brother, was sympathetic to Tucker. He said,

> The world is not a better place because the State of Texas executed Karla Faye Tucker. Even though Karla murdered my only sibling—my sister Deborah, who had raised me after our mother died—I stood with [Karla] as one of her witnesses when she was executed. . . . Karla and I had both done a lot of wrong in our lives. We had both turned to drugs to heal our pain; we had both hurt a lot of people. But the love of Jesus Christ transformed us. We were able to forgive ourselves and each other.

Allan Polunsky, chairman of the Texas Board of Criminal Justice, took another view, stating,

The issues here were not religious conversion or gender, but rather culpability and accountability. Karla Faye Tucker brutally murdered two innocent people and was found guilty by the court. . . . Although I believe she finally found God, her religious awakening could in no way excuse or mitigate her actions in the world she just left, but hopefully will provide her redemption in the world she just entered.

Just as supporters of the death penalty cite the Timothy McVeigh case, Karla Faye Tucker is a case for its opponents. Whereas McVeigh was unremorseful and unattractive to the public, Tucker was repentant and appealing. Her execution raised emotions and posed questions still debated today.

ALEJANDRO AVILA: CHILD MOLESTER AND MURDERER

Samantha Runnion was a lovely five-year-old who enjoyed drawing, singing, and decorating her bedroom with images of Peter Pan. She was happy and smiled a lot. On the evening of July 15, 2002, a mustached man kidnapped Samantha, taking her kicking and screaming as she played in front of her house. The following day, authorities found her body. An autopsy revealed she had been sexually assaulted, then choked to death. Factors in her case led police to fear her murder was the work of a serial rapist who would soon strike again.

Thanks to tips from the public and *forensics*, Alejandro Avila was arrested four days later and charged with kidnapping, murder, and sex crimes. Authorities had previously accused Avila of molesting two young girls, but that jury found him not guilty. This time, DNA and other evidence conclusively proved Avila's guilt in the rape and murder of little

Samantha Runnion. In the sentencing phase of the case, Avila's friends, family, and a local priest pleaded for his life, saying that his suffering as a child had changed him into a molester. Avila expressed no remorse for his crime. According to an article in the July 23, 2005, *Arizona Republic*, Erin Runnion, Samantha's mother, who had spent three years seeking justice for her daughter, confronted Avila, saying, "I know she looked at you with those amazing brown eyes and you still wanted to kill her. . . . I don't understand it and I never will." The judge concluded, "For the temporary gratification of his lust, the defendant destroyed an entire family's future, he has forfeited his right to live."

Because Avila was sentenced to death, his case will automatically be appealed, as are all death penalty sentences in the state of California. For Erin Runnion, Avila's death sentence is the justice she has sought over the past three years. Supporters of the death penalty point to cases such as this as proof of the death penalty's relevance.

Alejandro Avila after his arrest

Mumia Abu-Jamal was a radical, black activist who insists that he was framed by the Philadelphia police.

Abu-Jamal in his prison cell

MUMIA ABU-JAMAL: MURDERER OR VICTIM OF INJUSTICE?

The case of death row convict Mumia Abu-Jamal is emotional, controversial, and **divisive**. Defenders see Abu-Jamal as a political prisoner framed by the Philadelphia police, whereas others see him as a cold-blooded murderer. The Abu-Jamal case has attracted the attention of celebrities including Spike Lee, Maya Angelou, Alec Baldwin, and Susan Sarandon, as well as organizations as far away as France and Denmark. On the other hand, the chorus of pleas for Abu-Jamal's pardon infuriates family and friends of slain Philadelphia police officer Daniel Faulkner.

At 4 A.M. on December 9, 1981, police officer Daniel Faulkner stopped a car and arrested its driver, William Cook, for driving the wrong

direction in downtown Philadelphia. Shortly after that, other police officers arriving at the scene found Officer Faulkner dead in the street with bullets in his back and face. Nearby, Cook's brother, Mumia Abu-Jamal, lay wounded by a bullet from Officer Faulkner's gun. Abu-Jamal was already famous in Philadelphia as a *radical* black *activist* whose distrust of police stemmed from an incident years earlier when police officers had joined a group of racists who attacked and beat him.

At his trial, Abu-Jamal sought to defend himself. Denied the ability to do so, Abu-Jamal was defended by a court-appointed attorney. The jury found Abu-Jamal guilty of the murder of Office Daniel Faulkner and sentenced him to death. For the past twenty-two years, he has proclaimed his innocence and sought to escape the death penalty. Supporters of Abu-Jamal claim he should receive a new trial because of issues including ineffective counsel, the validity of witnesses, selection of the jury, actions of the jury, actions of the judge, and the *dubious* nature of items presented as evidence. Abu-Jamal's supporters believe the Philadelphia police framed the activist. However, those who support the death sentence given to Abu-Jamal are convinced the Philadelphia legal system conducted his trial properly. On June 16, 2005, the Pennsylvania Court of Appeals rejected Abu-Jamal's latest legal appeal, and as of the time of this writing, he is awaiting execution.

TORTURED BY POLICE, SENTENCED TO DEATH, PARDONED

On January 11, 2003, four men facing execution in Illinois—Aaron Patterson, Madison Hobley, Stanley Howard, and Leroy Orange—received the greatest gift imaginable: Illinois governor George Ryan granted them a full pardon. "I believe these men are innocent or I wouldn't have pardoned them," said the governor. "The system has failed for all four men and it has failed for all of the people of this state. . . . There isn't any doubt in my mind these four men were wrongfully prosecuted, and wrongfully sentenced to die." The four men had all been tortured by order of Chicago police commander John Burge, whom the city fired for his misconduct; at least sixty-six people claim they were tortured by Burge or police officers under his command. The governor's pardons came about as the result of research begun by journalism students at Northwestern University; the students were the first to discover the torture and false sentencing. All told, there have been seventeen death row cases overturned in Illinois in recent years. Cases such as this fuel opposition to the death penalty. If more than a dozen people can be wrongly sentenced to death in one state, then how many of the thousands of death row inmates across America might also be falsely sentenced to death?

The cases in this chapter represent the diversity and controversy of death row sentencing. Some convicts, such as mass murderer McVeigh or child killer Avila, draw public support for the death penalty as citizens find it difficult to sympathize with these criminals. Other death row inmates, such as Tucker and Abu-Jamal, have gathered widespread public support against the death penalty, due either to their perceived change of life or belief in their innocence. Cases such as that of the men pardoned in Illinois also present a challenge for the death penalty; they show that the system of justice sometimes errs and leads opponents of the death penalty to question how many wrongly convicted prisoners states may have executed. In the meantime, more than 3,500 persons in the United States await execution.

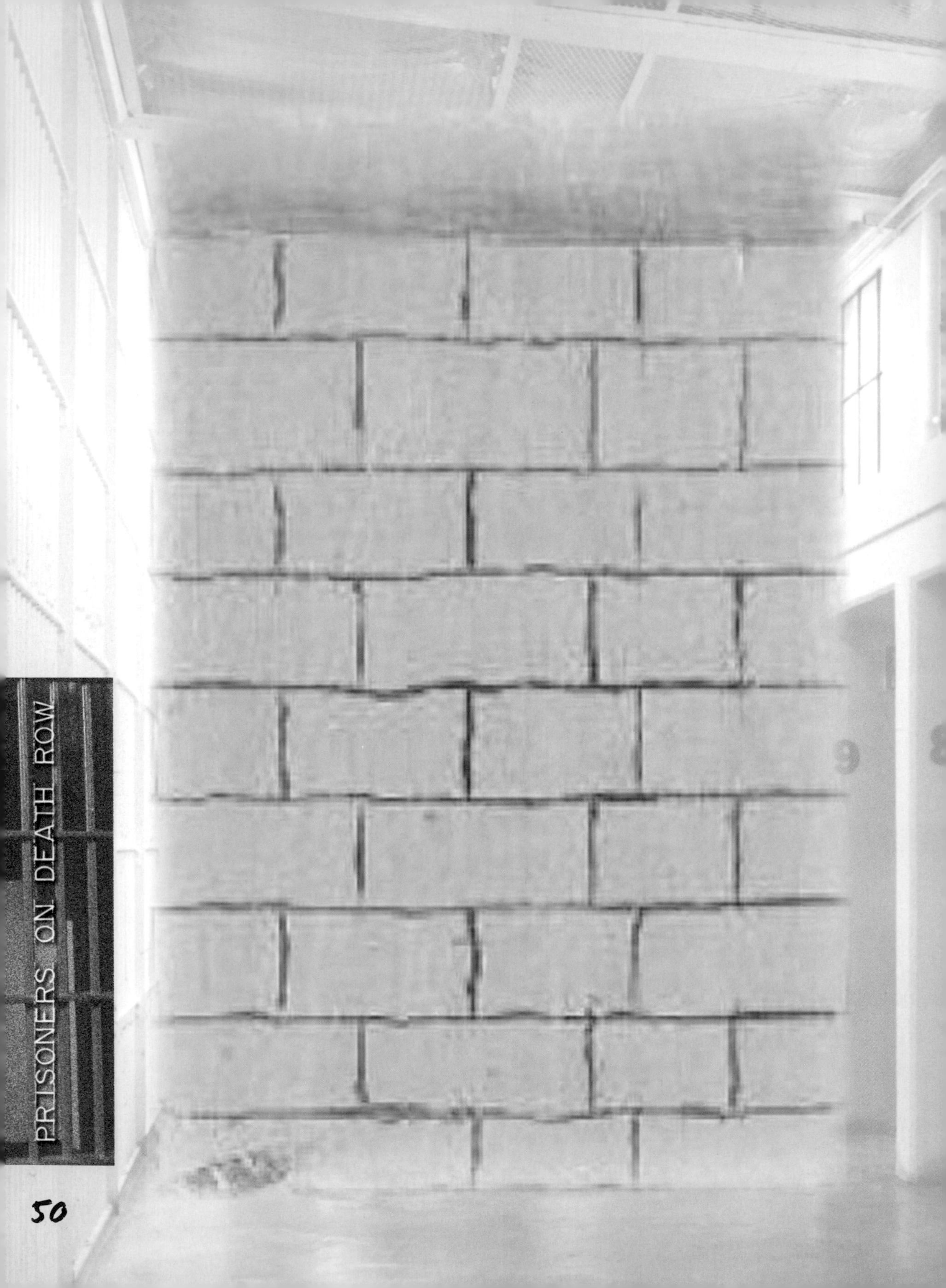
9

CHAPTER 3

LIFE ON DEATH ROW

"Basically, prison officials' 'program' for death row is designed to separate us from our humanity and dignity, while disrupting our access to outside resources and support." That is how Roger Buehl, a Pennsylvania death row inmate, describes life in prison awaiting execution. The average time between sentencing and execution is almost a decade, so most death row inmates live a long time as prisoners. They are kept in the strictest prisons where they are offered the least freedoms; public officials have few threats to hold over inmates already headed for execution (what can they do, double a death sentence?).

Supporters of the present system feel the strict rules and harsh conditions on death row are justified, both to prevent the very worst criminals from escaping and to punish them for their crimes. Some of the families of murder victims question why tax dollars should go to provide food and shelter for murderers, while they continue to suffer grief; according to some, it makes sense to feed and clothe death row inmates as cheaply and minimally as possible. At the same time, opponents of the death penalty argue that death row inmates are serving two sentences for the same crime—facing years of unhappiness in prison in addition to their sentence of death.

DEATH ROW FACILITIES

Increasingly, states hold death row inmates in "supermax" prisons designed to be virtually escape proof. Authorities design such facilities so that only one prisoner at a time is allowed outside his cell, and there is minimum exposure to outside air, light, and so on. These facilities rely on technology such as automatically opening or locking doors to enable a minimum number of guards to control the prisoners. One benefit of such strict facilities is minimizing prisoner-on-prisoner violence, a factor that threatens many inmates in less strict facilities.

Roger Buehl describes typical death row quarters in SCI (State Correctional Institution) in Greene, western Pennsylvania:

> We are kept in constant confinement, locked in-cell all day long—except for the five days a week we are allowed one whole hour outside (in another, slightly bigger, cage). Cell temperatures are kept cold and breezy by powerful forced-air vents, yet permissible clothing is limited. All meals are served in-cell, on a filthy tray shoved through a slot in the door. Showers? For us, it's three times weekly.

In his book *Waiting to Die*, Arizona death row inmate Richard Michael Rossi explains that authorities call the living areas in prison "pods"

Holding cells in San Quentin Prison where death row inmates wait for execution.

presumably because cells are lined up one after another, "like peas in a pod." There are ten cells to a pod (five lower and five upper) and six pods to a cluster, for a total of sixty cells. Every cell is observable from a central command tower by means of computers and TV monitors. Doors are opened electronically, and death row rules allow only one cell door to be opened at any one time. An intercom communicates with each cell.

Cells are plain rooms with unpainted walls, floor, and ceiling. In the Arizona facility where Rossi is held, there are no bars on the front of cells. Instead, solid walls with thousands of tiny holes in them allow the guards to see inside at all times. There is a bunk of welded steel with a thin plastic foam mattress and a chair welded to the floor. Death row rules allow inmates to have televisions and radios—their one luxury item—to keep them occupied and therefore less dangerous. While prisoners cannot touch one another, they can shout to each another from inside their cells, and what they are watching on television is the common topic of conversation.

The entrance to death row in a federal prison

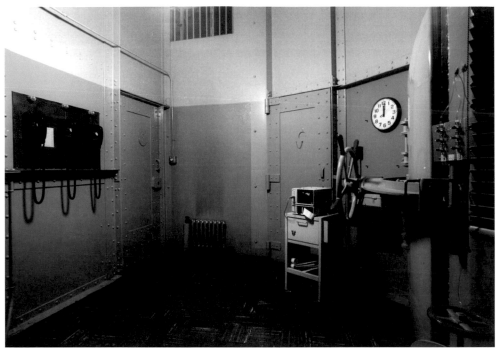

The anteroom outside the execution chamber in San Quentin Prison

Rossi describes prison smells:

> The first thing you notice when stepping inside any prison cell block is the putrid odor. All cell blocks smell, but they do not come close to death row. We all die a little bit each day on the row, and the odor accumulates and builds to an unbelievable level. . . . [Death row smells of] fear, anger, rancid sweat, blood, stale urine, wasted semen, feces and flatulence.

Rossi also describes the "fellow inmates" found on death row—field mice, scorpions, two-inch long sewer roaches, cockroaches, black widow spiders, various other insects, and "lots of mosquitoes" that come in through the holes or climb up through the drains.

Men call out to one another constantly, communicating by voice to make up for their lack of physical companionship. Some fight verbally, cussing and yelling at one another, while others check on the welfare of

Daily life on death row is bleak and dismal.

fellow prisoners. Rossi says, "The constant roar becomes a living, breathing entity of its own. It is not hard to go crazy from the din. . . . We decay and rot like unpicked fruit."

DAILY LIFE ON DEATH ROW

Five times a day there are "counts" by the prison staff to make sure no prisoner is dead or missing. The first count is at five A.M., at which time prisoners must stand up to show they are alive and accounted for. If any prisoner does not get up, a force of guards assembles to enter his cell and check on his condition. Guards punish prisoners who refuse to comply with the counts by detention in "the hole," a solitary cell with even more *spartan* furnishings.

Guards feed prisoners by means of trays loaded off food carts. To get his food, each prisoner must sit on his bunk, away from the opening so the guard knows it is safe to place the try there. The inmate must also place the tray back on its ledge when finished and sit away from the ledge so the prison staff can retrieve the tray. Failure to do so may result in a group of guards coming in the cell with riot gear and batons.

Prisons design death row meals to cost taxpayers the least possible amount of money, less than three dollars a day in Arizona. On Saturdays and Sundays, prisoners are fed only two meals daily. The mid-day meal is a sack lunch of inexpensive meat and bread. Fruits have been eliminated from Arizona death row diets to cut down on expenses. Rossi notes, "We are being fed diets of sugar-laden calories, high in starches and carbohydrates, empty of nutrition." This diet, combined with the lack of exercise on death row, causes inmates to become obese, giving the impression that prisoners are well fed; this is not the case. Rossi concludes, "We are being fed like cattle being fattened for the slaughter."

Three times a week, prisoners are allowed to exercise and shower. Exercise consists of an hour alone in a room larger than the cell, but "smaller than the average dog run." One at a time, guards allow prisoners to enter the exercise room, which contains no basketball hoop or workout equipment, only a small rubber ball the prisoner may bounce off the walls.

After the period of exercise, guards allow the prisoner a shower. He must strip and allow the guards to look under his arms, in his mouth, and under his testicles. Then, he enters the shower, "a nasty, musty smelling little closet measuring five by six feet. There are no windows . . . if you are claustrophobic, the shower is not the place for you."

For Rossi, the worst aspect of life in Arizona's death row prison is the lack of windows. He says, "Not having a window is one of the cruelest things that has been done to us. . . . We will never again be able to see the night sky, or a star, or the moon again."

PRISONERS' PRIVILEGES

Since authorities regard death row inmates as especially dangerous, they are given fewer privileges than are other inmates. Whereas most prison-

Death row inmates are allowed to exercise outside three times a week.

VOLUNTEERS FOR DEATH

We usually think of the word "volunteer" in connection with positive choices; people volunteer to help at a hospital, clean up a woods, and so on. However, the word "volunteer" has a grim meaning on death row. When someone volunteers there, it means they choose to give up the appeals process, hence they "volunteer" to be executed. Many death row inmates have chosen to volunteer because the prospect of death seems more pleasant than continuing to live with the unhappiness of daily life in harsh confinement.

ers are allowed to attend religious services, inmates on Arizona's death row are not allowed to assemble for religious worship as they cannot be in the same room at the same time. Religious observance is limited to volunteers who are allowed to stop in front of individual cells and converse with the inmates; these are not allowed to give any religious literature to the prisoners. Letters and writings of those on death row, whether they are religious or not, express appreciation for these volunteers as they are often their only form of contact with the outside world.

Health services are not easy for prisoners to attain, due at least in part to the tendency of some prisoners to abuse such services or attempt to escape when being taken from their cell for treatment. To receive medical care, a prisoner must submit a form that authorities must review and accept before he can see a medical worker. Before a medical exam, each prisoner is strip searched and chained to prevent escape. Nurse practitioners, rather than doctors, usually provide medical care in prisons. Since medical workers in prisons are paid less than those in outside

Conditions on death row often cause mental illness.

practices, they are sometimes less skilled than their counterparts outside the prison system. Authorities allow death row inmates to see outside specialists or receive help in hospitals very rarely, since these prisoners are considered high-escape risks. Rossi says, "I have seen at least six men die of cancer or other major illnesses because they were not diagnosed early enough. . . . One man died because the battery in his pacemaker gave out before it was replaced."

Conditions on death row cause numerous cases of mental illness. Authorities usually treat these with medications. After workers prescribe medication, death row inmates see a psychologist every month or so for a refill of medication; visits are brief with little discussion. There is no doctor–patient confidentiality as is legally required outside prison. Anything a death row inmate tells his doctor can be used against him in court.

Each death row prisoner is allowed to have ten people on his visitation list. These people are allowed to see him unless they have a criminal background. In-state visitors can come and visit once a week for two hours; out-of-state visitors can stay longer. Visits are "no contact," done by speaking through a window or screen. Members of the press or media are not allowed to conduct interviews with prisoners in the state of Arizona. Prison authorities may require visitors to undergo strip searches or vehicle searches if they suspect foul play.

There are reasons for the strict limitations on visitors. For example, visitors have brought drugs, guns, and other weapons into prisons under their tongues and in their body cavities. Therefore, following visits, prison guards strip search prisoners and then place them in a magnetometer chair that functions as a thorough, head-to-toe metal detector.

Although inmates on death row are physically isolated from the outside world and might seem very alone, there are people on the outside who have committed themselves to influencing the fates of these inmates—either for death or release.

CHAPTER 4

VICTIMS' FAMILIES AND ACTIVISTS

We have become so liberal and so worried about the criminal that the victim means nothing any more. . . . Well, let me tell you, all these women who were murdered meant a lot to all of us and the community, and we have to show people that you cannot commit these crimes without paying for what you do.

The speaker was Lynne Marino, and she was testifying before a joint meeting of the Louisiana State Senate Judiciary and State House Criminal Justice committees in December of 2003. Marino had good reason for her feelings; her daughter, Pam

Kinamore, was one of seven women believed killed by serial killer Derrick Todd Lee between 2002 and 2003. The hearings were set to determine if Lee was eligible to receive the death penalty for his crimes. The Baton Rouge Advocate.com recorded statements at the hearing.

Another speaker at the hearing was Ann Pace, the mother of another of Lee's victims. Pace told the panel how the brutal murder of her daughter, Charlotte Murray Pace, forced her to deal with the reality of violence. She said, "In an ideal world, I would not have a picture in my head this Christmas that involves the incredibly battered and brutalized body of my daughter in a plastic bag on a metal table." Pace concluded that the only way to keep others safe from Lee would be his execution, since "I don't think anyone on earth claims that there is rehabilitation for serial murderers."

In October of the following year, a Louisiana jury took only ninety-three minutes to recommend the death sentence for Lee for the brutal murder of Charlotte Murray Pace, in spite of defense witness testimony that Lee is mentally retarded. DNA evidence connected Lee to the seven murders in Louisiana. While Lee is on death row, the victims' families continue to struggle with the pain of their loss. The mother of one victim struggles with her emotions, saying, "I vowed not to let Derrick Todd Lee kill me too, but he has killed my hopes and dreams for happiness."

The most powerful defense of the death penalty comes not from professors or judges but from the families of murder victims. Many of the mothers, fathers, husbands, or siblings whose loved ones were slain make impassioned pleas stating their need for justice. For these survivors, justice means the execution of the killer.

The pain of victims' families, and the desire to see justice for them, can also motivate the lawyers who prosecute death penalty cases. In October 2002, the *San Pablo Avenue Times* described prosecutor Angela Backers. She typically works eighty hours a week, for a full year, on death penalty cases. What motivates her to work so hard? It isn't the pay. She describes working on a case involving a serial rapist and murderer: "You become very close to the family. . . . You treat their tragedy as your own." She experiences times of "physical, intellectual and emotional" exhaustion, but concludes, "if justice is done, then it's all worth it."

DNA evidence was used to convict serial killer Derrick Todd Lee.

An electric chair is a simple but deadly device. When the chair malfunctions, however, it can amount to torture.

OTHER FAMILY OPINIONS

On March 24, 1997, the state of Florida executed Pedro Medina, a Cuban national. The state's electric chair, nicknamed "Old Sparky," sent 2,000 volts of electricity into his body, and the smell of burning flesh filled the execution chamber. Michael Minerva, Medina's lawyer, witnessed the execution: "It was brutal, terrible. . . . It was a burning alive, literally." The malfunctioning electric chair was not the only controversy in the case. Though a jury convicted Medina of killing a former neighbor, some people—most notably, the victim's daughter, Lindi James—questioned his guilt. James said she never believed Medina killed her mother; she also stated that her mother would not want Medina executed, even if guilty.

Lindi James is by no means unique in her plea against the death penalty for her mother's alleged killer. In 1993, eighteen-year-old Joseph Shadow Clark murdered Paul Bosco's brother John, along with his wife, Nancy. Paul Bosco has stated:

> One of the great counterarguments death penalty opponents face is the challenge, "If it were your spouse/child/sibling who was murdered, you'd feel differently." Never did I feel that that boy's shocked parents, who were losing their son as surely as my parents lost theirs, and who have the added pain of shame, needed to suffer more. An 18-year-old's execution would not give back the dead. Nor would it have given me "closure," which I regard as a myth—a politician's fiction. Spare me, please, your feel-good vengeance.

Likewise, the victim's mother, Antoinette Bosco, argues, "The pain of losing a loved one by the horrible act of murder is not lessened by the horrible murder of another, not even when it is cloaked as 'justice' and state-sanctioned. It is only a delusion to believe that one's pain is ended by making someone else feel pain." Joseph Shadow Clark was sentenced to prison rather than execution.

On December 22, 1986, James Bernard Campbell entered a church and stabbed Reverend Billy Bosler, twenty-four times. The pastor's daughter, SueZann, attempted to save her father, but Campbell stabbed her on her head and back and left her for dead. SueZann lay on the floor struggling for life, listening to Campbell *pillage* the church and watching her father die. Later, when Campbell came to trial, SueZann recalled her father's favorite hymn, "Let There Be Peace on Earth," specifically the line "Let there be peace on earth, and let it begin with me." She was determined to spare Campbell from the death penalty, believing that doing so would honor her father's wishes. For ten years, throughout three trials and two sentencings, Bosler worked to save the life of her father's murderer. One Florida judge threatened SueZann Bosler with contempt of court for her position in favor of Campbell's life. Finally, on June 13, 1977, SueZann's efforts were successful; the state of Florida commuted Campbell's death sentence to four consecutive life terms. She said the killer's reprieve was like "a weight lifted from my shoulders." SueZann Bosler recently received permission to visit Campbell in jail.

LEAST RECOGNIZED VICTIMS

Though they do not always raise their voices, the families of executed criminals also suffer in death penalty cases. In the face of public anger over the crime, they are sometimes reluctant to give voice to their suffering, but executions affect them also.

Bill Babbitt made a difficult decision, one that has haunted him ever since. Bill's brother Manuel (Manny) came home from Vietnam suffering from posttraumatic stress disorder, and Bill tried to help him. One night, experiencing flashbacks of the war, Manny broke into a home and killed an elderly woman, Leah Schendel. Grief-stricken, Bill went to the police and told them what Manny had done, hoping to protect others from what his brother might do and also hoping to get help for his brother's

The execution chamber in San Quentin Prison where Manny Babbitt was put to death by lethal injection.

mental problems. The police said Manny would not get the death penalty and promised help for his mental illness. But, instead, Manuel Babbitt received the death penalty. In March of 1998, while he served time on death row, the U.S. government awarded the Purple Heart to Babbitt for wounds he received in the Vietnam War thirty years before. Then, on May 4, 1999, the state of California executed Manuel Babbitt by lethal injection in San Quentin State Prison.

Bill Babbitt told Susannah Sheffer of MVFR that he felt like killing himself after his brother's execution, but instead he chooses to live and oppose the death penalty. Sheffer writes:

> Bill turned his brother in because he didn't want any more violence. He didn't get that. He turned his brother in because he wanted help, and he didn't get that either. . . . Bill and others like him are murder victims' family members too . . . judicial executions . . . leave relatives who have to bury their dead and grieve for them.

The mother of another executed prisoner described her anguish this way: "I never felt such pain as I did the night that my son died. I didn't think I would live through it, and I am not sure that I wanted to. . . . I sincerely hope that no other mother will have to go through that kind of pain again."

AN AWARD-WINNING ACTIVIST

Sister Helen Prejean, member of a Catholic religious order, is perhaps the best-known activist working on behalf of death row inmates. Born on April 21, 1939, in Baton Rouge, Louisiana, Sister Prejean joined the Sisters of St. Joseph in 1957. In 1981, Sister Prejean dedicated her life to the poor of New Orleans, and at that time she began her prison ministry. As a result, she became pen pals with Patrick Sonnier, the convicted killer

MURDER VICTIMS FOR RECONCILIATION

Murder Victims for Reconciliation (MVFR) is a national organization of murder victims' families' who oppose the death penalty. According to their Web site,

> Our members are people who have come to believe that our own grief will not be lessened by causing pain to others. Executions create more grieving families, and loved ones of the executed within our membership join together for support and to express their opposition to the death penalty.

They publish the book *Not in Our Name*, which includes scores of statements from the families of murder victims opposing the death penalty, along with the family members' pictures and stories.

of two teenagers, who was sentenced to die in Louisiana's electric chair. Serving as his spiritual adviser, Sister Prejean repeatedly visited Sonnier on death row. In a recent speech, she explained her feelings after seeing the execution:

> When I witnessed the killing of Patrick Sonnier in Louisiana's electric chair on April 5, 1984, I left the execution chamber traumatized. Driving home afterwards we had to stop the car because I had to vomit. I could hardly believe that I had just witnessed my state government killing a human being in such a deliberate and calculated protocol of death. I realized that very few people were ever going to be allowed to witness what I had witnessed, and

Sister Helen Prejean, advocate for both death row inmates and their victims

There is suffering on both sides of the prison bars.

from that moment, my mission was born. I had been a witness so I must tell the story, I must be the one to take people on the spiritual journey I had taken so they could be brought face to face with government killing.

Sister Helen turned her experiences into a book, *Dead Man Walking*, which was nominated for a 1993 Pulitzer Prize, was number one on the *New York Times* Best Seller List for thirty-one weeks, and was an international best seller, translated into ten different languages. In 1996, *Dead Man Walking* became an Oscar-winning major motion picture, starring Susan Sarandon as Sister Helen (she won the Oscar for Best Performance by an Actress) and Sean Penn as a death row inmate. In 2000, it became an opera that has played to critical acclaim for five years.

Sister Helen Prejean works both with death penalty inmates, and their victims. She explains: "In taking people on this journey from vengeance to compassion, I am careful to bring them over to both sides of

According to the Gospel account, the centurion at the foot of the cross declared, "This man is innocent." Centurion Ministries follows this philosophy, and has freed more than twenty-five men and women who would otherwise have been executed.

the issue: the suffering of the victims' family and their search for healing on one side and the suffering of the condemned and his or her family on the other."

CENTURION MINISTRIES

Jim McCloskey calls himself "missionary to the despised"; his life pursuit is justice for death row inmates who are innocent. He calls his organization Centurion Ministries, named after the centurion who, at the foot of Jesus's cross, exclaimed, "This man is innocent." As of 2005, McCloskey's efforts over two decades have brought freedom to more than twenty-five men and women formerly awaiting execution.

Centurion Ministries works to free innocent prisoners.

By his time he had reached his thirties, McCloskey was a wealthy businessperson, but it troubled him that he was "living a shallow, selfish, superficial, inauthentic life." After selling his possessions and quitting his job, he enrolled at Princeton Theological Seminary, intending to become a minister. While studying in the seminary, McCloskey visited prisoners at Trenton State Prison. There he met Jorge De Los Santos, a former drug addict convicted of murder, who insisted he was innocent. Against the advice of his friends, McCloskey took two years off from school to investigate De Los Santos' claims, using up his savings and a $10,000 loan from his parents. McCloskey's determined efforts caused the state to reexamine the case, and De Los Santos was eventually proven innocent and released. This success started Jim McCloskey on the road to Centurion Ministries.

McCloskey and Centurion Ministries' staff of five rely on private donations for funding. They go through 1,300 requests for help each year and take on three new cases annually. These cases are only pursued after a review lasting an average of five years; McCloskey and the staff of Centurion Ministries want to be sure each client is innocent. According to McCloskey, there are several reasons authorities wrongfully convict people of murder: sometimes police and prosecutors withhold evidence, prosecutors may rely on jailhouse snitches, and often detectives fail to investigate adequately.

One of the prisoners freed by Centurion Ministries was Clarence Brandley, who spent ten years on Texas's death row for a 1980 Conroe, Texas, rape and murder. On the eve of his execution in 1990, Centurion Ministries brought forward an eyewitness to the crime, who named the real killers and cleared Brandley of the murder charge. Kerry Max Cook is another falsely convicted death row inmate freed through the efforts of Centurion Ministries. Cook spent nearly twenty years on death row convicted of a murder he did not commit. In 1997, after a grueling seven-year effort by Centurion Ministries on Cook's behalf, the State of Texas threw out his conviction, admitting "illicit manipulation of the evidence permeated the entire investigation of the murder," and that the state "gained a conviction based on fraud and ignored its own duty to seek the truth."

Despite their determined efforts, Centurion Ministries' investigations do not always succeed in freeing their clients. The State of Louisiana executed Jimmy Wingo by electric chair on June 16, 1987. Prior to that, McCloskey obtained videotaped **recantations** by the two main state witnesses, who admitted a deputy sheriff coerced them into lying at Wingo's trial. However, a dismissive Louisiana governor and Board of Pardons rejected this strong evidence. Centurion Ministries remains convinced the State of Louisiana executed an innocent man.

As we have seen, the death penalty involves more lives than just that of the convicted murderer; the death penalty affects the families of the victims and the families of death row inmates, lawyers, and activists who become involved with inmates' lives. It even affects the prison guards and wardens.

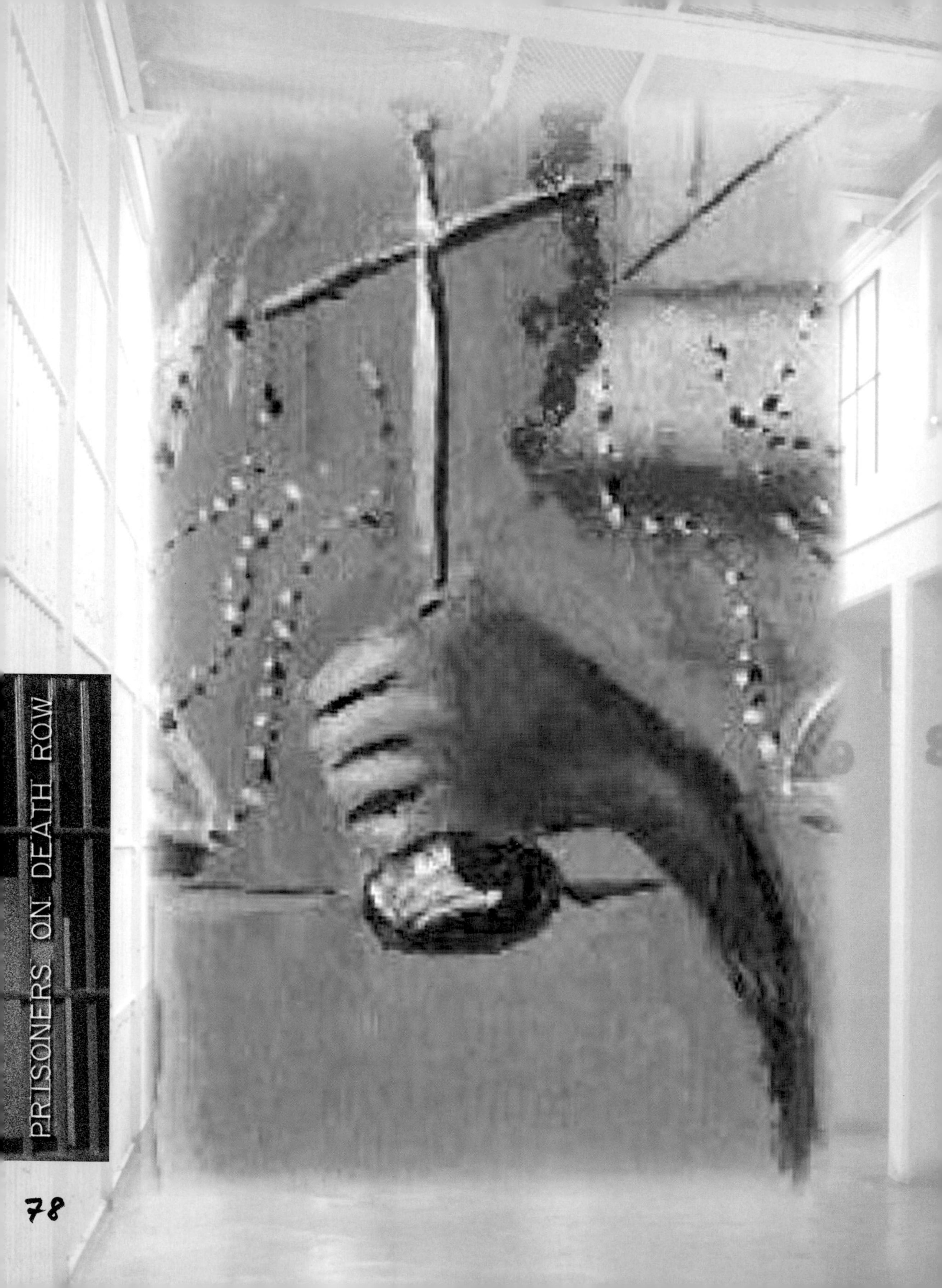

CHAPTER 5

GUARDS AND EXECUTIONERS

"Now it is a terrible business to mark out a man for the vengeance of man," said British philosopher G. K. Chesterton. If his statement is true, then we should expect that those persons who work on death row and those who conduct executions would struggle with their work. In fact, books offer little information regarding the thoughts and feelings of death row guards and executioners. Such workers value **anonymity** as a safeguard from criminals who might try to get at them in order to assist inmates, and from harassment by the public.

PRISON GUARDS

The Last Face You'll Ever See, by Ivan Solotaroff, is an unusually intimate look inside the private lives of several prison officials who oversaw Mississippi's death row. The book is not comprehensive in its scope; it focuses on two men—Donald Cabana, who later became an activist against the death penalty, and Donald Hocutt, who had a falling out with the state over his request for medical payments—and they may not be representative of all the people who hold such jobs. However, the book offers a **candid** look into the lives of public defenders charged with enforcing the death penalty.

Solotaroff describes Hocutt's first impressions when he began working with convicted murderers at the Parchman Maximum Security Unit (MSU), which included the state's death row population. His first impression was "a horrible smell, half chemical, half institutional . . . as he walked the MSU's length the first time." One of his first jobs was serving medications to the inmates by placing trays in the slots of their cells. Another guard warned Hocutt not to mix up anyone's medications lest he

Prison guards endure intense psychological stress.

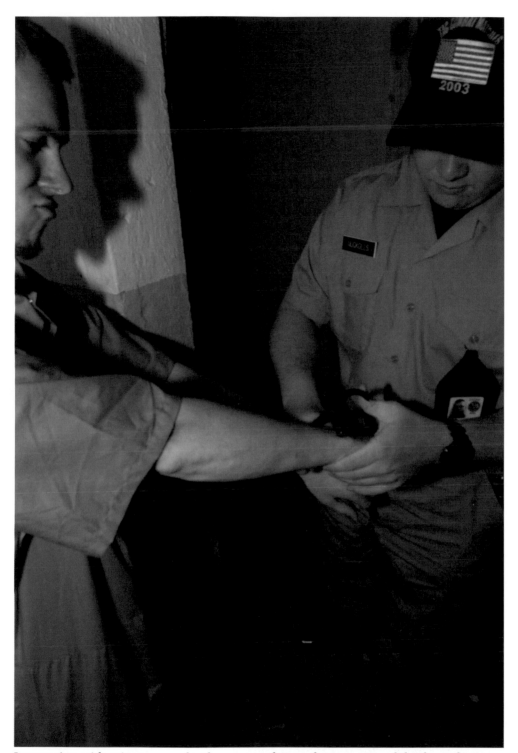

Interaction with prisoners on death row can change the way a guard thinks and acts.

Some guards may experience a sense of exhilaration from being able to have the upper hand over prisoners.

face "a king-sized federal lawsuit." Prisoners threw feces, urine, and other disgusting things at the guards as they placed the trays in their slots.

Although the job involved frequent conflicts, Solotaroff says Hocutt soon discovered he felt a sort of exhilaration "knowing he had the advantage over these people." In the outside world, they were powerful, frightening—they had committed murders—but inside these walls, "they were behind bars and he had the key."

Literature on prison workers commonly suggests severe stress affects them, and they thus become "hardened" or "*desensitized*" in order to cope with their work. However, research published by Howard Osofsky in June of 2001, suggests otherwise. Osofsky is senior mental health consultant for Louisiana's Angola Prison, the setting for the book and movie *Dead Man Walking*. He is also chairperson of the psychiatry department at Louisiana State University School of Medicine in New Orleans. Between 1999 and 2001, Osofsky interviewed fifty death row staffers

Constant exposure to prisoners' suffering may desensitize guards.

Many guards see themselves as "soldiers of the court."

REFLECTIONS OF A FORMER DEATH ROW CORRECTIONAL OFFICER

Lorie J. Hopper, a former death row correctional officer, writes on a Web site called placesoftheheart.com:

It was really hard work; physically & mentally. There was a very fine line between trying to do the job fairly and not being too "friendly." It was hard to be treated differently by male staff & inmates. . . . Just because I was a female, only 5'3" in height was no reason why I couldn't do the same work as the male officers. . . . The day-to-day work was mostly routine and generally uneventful. I didn't spend much time pondering upon the fact that I was working in the midst of persons who had been, at the very least, convicted of capital murder. I saw regular human beings, many of whom had their "knucklehead moments" at times. But I saw people smile, laugh, cry, fight, etc.

including officers who process newly arriving inmates, guards, and executioners. He wanted to learn how the stress of working on death row affected these men and women.

Osofsky found death row workers were not motivated by a desire to take revenge against criminals. He says, "They describe themselves instead as 'soldiers of the court,'" responsible for carrying the sentences ordered by judges and juries. Furthermore, Osofsky says that death row workers "place a high value on treating their charges as people," even if

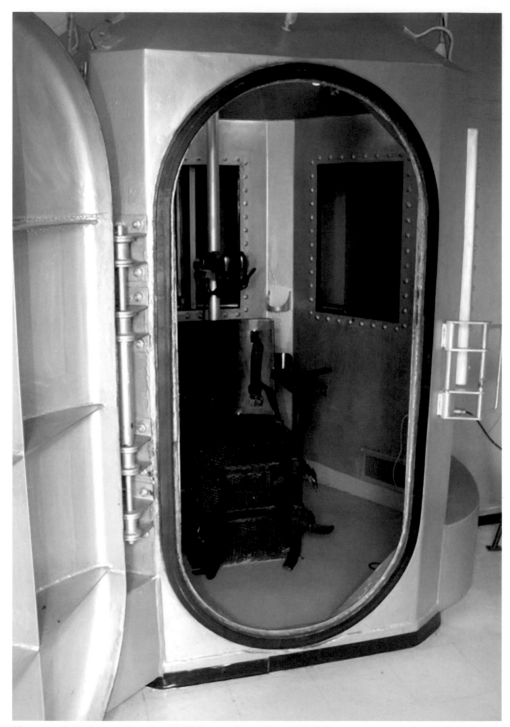

The gas chamber at Parchman Prison where Donald Cabana was superintendent in the 1980s.

Death row in Stateville Prison

the inmates have committed **reprehensible** murders. He also found "the vast majority of staff are very religious." How does the job of executing an inmate influence those who perform such work? One officer told Osofsky, "If anybody says executions don't impact themselves, there's something wrong with them." Another admitted, "After it is over, you get to thinking about [the inmate]. You try to block out what happened, but you can't—his death is there." To cope, Osofsky says, "they stopped thinking about the execution when they left the prison gates. They had done their part, and it was time to move on."

A DEATH ROW SUPERINTENDENT'S TALE

As related in *The Last Face You'll Ever See*, Donald Cabana became superintendent of Mississippi's Parchman MSU in October of 1984, and he oversaw two executions that took place while he held this post. The first man executed under his orders was Edward Earl Johnson, a black man convicted of killing a white police officer. Johnson insisted the local sheriffs had "simply taken the first nigger they could find" and framed him as the murderer. Johnson's fellow inmates were unanimous in asserting his innocence, a practically unheard of phenomenon on death row.

Shortly before Johnson's execution, Cabana asked if he needed *Valium* to face the gas chamber. The condemned man refused the sedative, saying, "I want a clear mind when you walk me in there," and then ask-

The execution witness area in San Quentin Prison, where witnesses can observe death by lethal injection.

ing the superintendent, "Will you be needing one for yourself?" When Cabana replied in the negative, Johnson told him, "Good. I want you to have a clear mind, too . . . I want you to remember every last detail, because I'm innocent, Mr. Cabana. I'm innocent."

The details of Johnson's execution, as recalled in Solotaroff's book, were not pretty. He describes its effect on Superintendent Cabana: "By the end, Cabana was well on his way to regarding what had happened not as a warden-insider running the thing but as an outsider, an abolitionist." The next morning he struggled, thinking of returning to work.

Cabana soon had to oversee another execution, that of Connie Ray Evans, described by Solotaroff as "a thin, handsome young man with a pencil mustache, a ten-gallon afro, and a personable, peaceful smile." A jury had sentenced Evans to death for the 1981 murder of Arun Phwa, a young shop clerk. Cabana and Evans shared a common religious faith and spent so much time conversing that, by the day of Evans' execution, Cabana felt he was killing a friend.

Just before the execution, Cabana asked Evans if he wished to make a final statement. Evans said, "I do have something to say, but I want to say it privately to you." Cabana stepped forward, and Connie Ray Evans told him, "From one Christian to another, I love you. You can bet I'm going to tell the Man how good you are."

After that, Donald Cabana struggled to command Evans' death. Finally, he yelled, "Do it," and the chamber filled with lethal gas; it took fifteen agonizing minutes for Evans to die. Leaving the death chamber, Cabana told his wife, "No more. I don't want to do this anymore."

We have considered death row from a variety of angles, including the statistics and history, of the murder cases, of victims, abolitionists, workers, and superintendents. One more perspective remains: a death row inmate's.

CHAPTER 6

FINAL MOMENTS

What is it like to face execution? This chapter looks at the process from a death row inmate's point of view.

APPEALS

As the date of execution draws closer, the lawyer who is representing you, probably on a **_pro bono_** basis to get a last-minute reprieve, visits more frequently. You fill out forms for a **clemency** hearing, stating why you believe you are entitled to a sentence change, what your involvement in the crime was, how you have changed, and what plans you have for the future. In the meantime, your lawyer is attempting to contact people who know you and are willing to speak with a review board, explaining how you have changed and are no longer a threat to society. He also has left messages with the governor, who may if he wishes grant you a pardon.

You have been on the "countdown" to execution twice before now and survived until this point. However, this time you have come to the

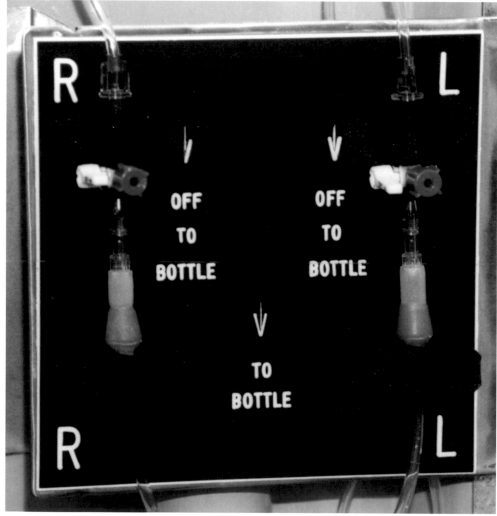

The lethal injection controls in San Quentin.

Waiting for death

After an execution, the body is released to the family for burial.

end of your appeals; there are no new cards to play. When all appeals
have been exhausted (save for the possibility of a last-second pardon
from the governor), they put you on deathwatch.

FILLING OUT FORMS

The reality of your approaching death comes home more as you fill out
the various related paperwork. First, there is a form for the disposition of
your property. Since you do not have many personal items at the prison,

this is not too difficult to do. Likewise, your last will and testament is not too hard either, as you have no investments, only a few dollars you have earned working in prison. Then you fill out the disposition of remains. If you have a wife or children, your body will be released to their chosen funeral home for burial after the execution. If you have no family, or if they choose not to claim your remains, you will be buried with a plain marker in a cemetery on the prison grounds. Finally, the day before your execution, there is the famous last meal request, a custom so ancient that no one is certain when or where it first started. After years of plain prison fare, you can order practically anything you want for your final supper.

AN EXTENDED VISIT WITH FAMILY

On the day of your execution, the prison allows you to visit for a few hours with your immediate family. Under any other circumstances, this would be a wonderful thing, because for a decade now, you have not been allowed to touch a visitor, only speak to them through a bulletproof screen, and you have never had more than one visitor at a time. Now, the prison allows you to be in the same room with your closest family, though only you are shackled to a chair and armed guards stand close around you. Authorities have ordered that the visit must end hours before midnight, which is the scheduled time of your execution, because they have learned things get too emotional with families as the execution nears. The hardest part of this visit is the very end, when you say your last good-bye to loved ones.

RELIGIOUS ADVISER

You eat your last meal, though you do not feel very hungry and actually just eat a portion of it. Then, if you are like many other prisoners facing

The deathwatch cell at San Quentin

DEATHWATCH

Deathwatch is the three-day period before execution during which the prison follows strict guidelines to make sure the inmate goes to death smoothly. Prison personnel are especially concerned that he does not attempt suicide. Inmates are put in a cell next to the execution chamber and placed under twenty-four-hour observation by a team of correctional officers who work twelve-hour shifts. The new cell is approximately eight feet by ten feet (2.5 meters by 3 meters) and contains a metal-framed bed with one mattress, a metal desk with an attached metal bench, a shower, a stainless steel sink, and toilet. Unlike the death row cell, this one has a small window, which provides a limited view of the prison grounds.

execution, you accept the opportunity to have the company of a religious adviser during your final hours. Although you still hope and pray for a last-minute reprieve from the governor, you have the increasing feeling that it's not going to happen. Over these past days, you have thought a lot about the next life and where you are headed. Your situation is unique because most people don't know when death will catch them, but you know only too well. Even though you think you are ready, it helps to have a spiritual counselor there to comfort you.

A prisoner's spiritual adviser can offer comfort before the prisoner's execution.

The execution chamber

THE EXECUTION CHAMBER

It is now less than an hour from your appointed death. Guards ask your spiritual adviser to step out of the room. You change into a fresh pair of prison clothes, under which you wear a diaper; when you die you will lose control of your bladder. Orderlies accompanied by guards bring a **gurney** into the room. Every part of your body is strapped very securely to the gurney using Velcro straps. If you are fortunate, they place two intravenous tubes into your arms; if you are unfortunate and have abused drugs to the extent that you have collapsed your veins, they will shave your legs near the groin and insert the intravenous tubes there. In the worst-case scenario, the orderlies use a scalpel to cut into your arm or leg to locate a vein. This is especially frustrating because you know these workers are not physicians—the **Hippocratic oath** taken by all doctors

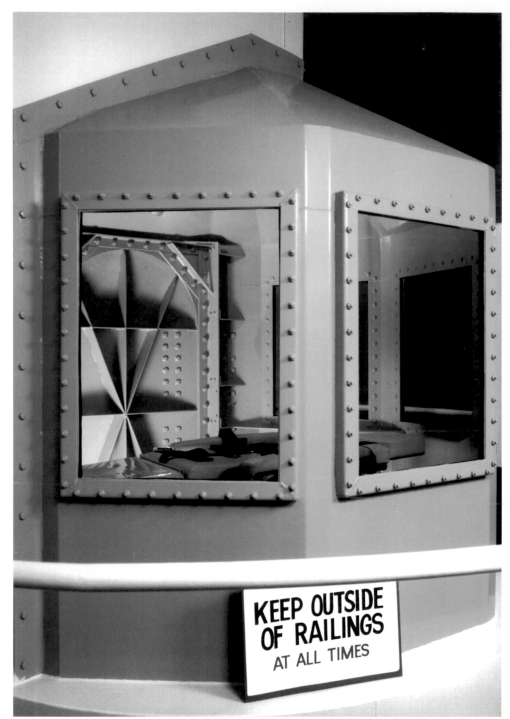

KEEP OUTSIDE
OF RAILINGS
AT ALL TIMES

Windows allow the person being executed to see out into the adjoining room where witnesses are watching.

prohibits them from participation in executions. You have heard stories of inmates whom prison workers cut up painfully in frustrated attempts to locate a suitable entry point for the intravenous tubes.

LAST WORDS

The orderlies wheel you into the execution chamber, a sterile-looking room with a window to an adjoining room. Through the window, you see your family, your spiritual adviser, your attorney, a few members of the press, and your victims' families. The prison warden asks if you have any final words. You do. The gurney is designed so the guards can push it upright, and they do so, allowing you to stand facing the audience for the execution. You have thought a lot about these words: what will you say? Will you say you are sorry for the pain you have caused the victims' families, will you speak of the afterlife that awaits you, or will you hurl bitter defiance at the people who are about to take your life? You glance at the faces behind the glass, the last faces you will ever see.

THE END

You can see the clock on the wall as the second hand reaches midnight. The red "hotline" phone has remained silent; there has been no last-minute call from the governor. The moment has come, and you know with certainty there will be no reprieve. The warden nods to the orderlies. They take out hypodermic needles from the cart. You wonder what it will actually feel like: some say it is quick and painless, others claim the first two drugs render you unable to move or speak, but you still feel pain as your internal organs stop working. No one has ever lived to tell, and you wonder which it will be.

An orderly takes a hypodermic full of the anesthesia sodium pentothal and injects it into your vein. Another orderly injects a syringe filled with Pavulon, a muscle relaxant that causes your lungs to stop breathing.

Does capital punishment serve the demands of justice?

Then comes the third injection, potassium chloride, which stops your heart, and . . .

The issue of capital punishment is complex and emotional. It is important for everyone to learn about all sides of the issue and reach their own conclusions. The decision of some nations to use the death penalty—as well as the decisions of many nations not to use the death penalty—have been based on the desires of the respective nations' citizens. It is the responsibility of each citizen to become an informed participant in the decisions made by government, including those involving life or death.

What do you think?

GLOSSARY

activist: A person who takes concrete action to bring about change.

anonymity: The state of being unnamed or unidentified.

appellate: Having to do with a system of appeals that reviews the judgment of another court.

arbitrary: Depending on individual choice.

barbarous: Showing extreme cruelty.

candid: Fair, free from bias.

capital punishment: Execution as the punishment for someone convicted of committing a crime.

clemency: Mercy.

closure: A sense of finality.

commute: Reduce a legal sentence to a less severe one.

desensitized: Become less sensitive to something, so that one is no longer emotionally affected.

deterrence: A means of discouraging an action.

divisive: Causing disagreement or hostility.

discriminately: To be done in a way that identifies subtle differences.

dubious: Likely to be dishonest or inaccurate.

ethicists: People who study ethics or are devoted to ethical ideals.

euthanasia: The act or practice of killing someone who has an incurable illness or injury, or allowing or assisting that person to die.

evangelical: Belonging to a Protestant Christian church whose members believe in the authority of the Bible and salvation through the personal acceptance of Jesus Christ.

forensics: The application of science to decide questions arising from crime or litigation.

guillotine: A machine used to execute people by cutting off their heads.

gurney: A wheeled stretcher used to transport medical patients.

Hippocratic oath: An oath taken by graduating doctors to observe the ethical standards of their profession.

industrialized: To adapt to industrial methods of production and manufacturing.

liberal: Having to do with a political perspective that emphasizes individual freedoms.

pariah: An outcast.

pillage: To rob a place using force, especially during war.

plea bargain: To make arrangements to reduce a sentence by pleading guilty to a lesser crime.

pro bono: Done for free, especially in reference to legal services.

radical: Extreme.

recantations: The taking back of testimony or confessions.

reprehensible: Highly unacceptable.

spartan: Lacking in luxury or comfort.

unrepentant: Not sorry.

Valium: Trademark name for diazepam, a tranquilizing drug used to reduce anxiety and tension, and as a muscle relaxant.

FURTHER READING

Banks, Deena. *Amnesty International*. Milwaukee, Wis.: World Almanac Library, 2004.

Banner, Stuart. *The Death Penalty: An American History*. Cambridge, Mass.: Harvard University Press, 2002.

Bessler, John D. *Kiss of Death: America's Love Affair with the Death Penalty*. Boston: Northeastern University Press, 2003.

Cabana, Donald. *Death at Midnight: Confessions of an Executioner*. Boston: Northeastern University Press, 1998.

Morris, Norval, and David J. Rothman. *The Oxford History of the Prison: The Practice of Punishment in Western Society*. New York: Oxford University Press, 1995.

Murder Victims' Families for Reconciliation (editors). *Not in Our Name: Murder Victims' Families Speak Out Against the Death Penalty*. Cambridge, Mass.: MVFR, 2003.

Prejean, Helen. *Dead Man Walking*. New York: Vintage, 1994.

Prejean, Helen. *The Death of Innocents: An Eyewitness Account of Wrongful Executions*. New York: Random House, 2005.

Rossi, Richard Michael. *Waiting to Die: Life on Death Row*. London: Vision, 2004.

Solotaroff, Ivan. *The Last Face You'll Ever See: The Private Life of the American Death Penalty*. New York: HarperCollins, 2001.

FOR MORE INFORMATION

Amnesty International's death penalty site
www.amnestyinternational.org/abolish

Centurion Ministries site
www.centurionministries.org

Death penalty abolitionist site
www.nodeathpenalty.org

General information on the death penalty
www.deathpenaltyinfo.org

List of U.S. death penalty cases
www.clarkprosecutor.org/html/death/usexecute.htm

Murder Victims' Families for Reconciliation
www.mvfr.org

Pro-death penalty site
www.prodeathpenalty.com

Sister Helen Prejean's official site
www.prejean.org

Step-by-step explanation of the execution process, with pictures
people.howstuffworks.com/lethal-injection.htm

Tour of death row
wpni01.auroraquanta.com/pv/deathrow

Publisher's note:
The Web sites listed on this page were active at the time of publication.
The publisher is not responsible for Web sites that have changed their
addresses or discontinued operation since the date of publication. The
publisher will review and update the Web-site list upon each reprint.

BIBLIOGRAPHY

"A Manifest Justice Has Occurred." http://www.stopcapitalpunishment. org/coverage/35.html.

Amnesty International USA. http://www.amnestyusa.org/abolish/dp_ qa.html.

Bessler, John D. *Kiss of Death: America's Love Affair with the Death Penalty.* Boston, Mass.: Northeastern University Press, 2003.

Centurion Ministries. http://www.centurionministries.org.

Death Penalty quotes by victims' families. http://people.freenet.de/ dpinfo/victimsfamilies.htm.

Helen Prejean, CSJ. http://www.prejean.org.

Memorial to Karla Faye Tucker Brown. http://www.geocities.com/ RainForest/Canopy/2525/karlamain.html.

Murder Victims Families for Reconciliation, eds. *Not in Our Name: Murder Victims' Families Speak Out Against the Death Penalty.* Cambridge, Mass.: Author, 2003.

Patrick Poland. http://www.clarkprosecutor.org/html/death/US/ poland621.htm.

Rossi, Richard Michael. *Waiting to Die: Life on Death Row.* London: Vision, 2004.

Sheffer, Susannah. "Justifiable Homicide." http://www.afsc.org/ pwork/0104/010420.htm.

Solotaroff, Ivan. *The Last Face You'll Ever See: The Private Life of the American Death Penalty.* New York: HarperCollins, 2001.

Timothy McVeigh. http://www.crimelibrary.com/serial_killers/ notorious/mcveigh/superstars_9.html?sect=1.

INDEX

PICTURE CREDITS

Chapter opening art was taken from a painting titled *Justice Denied* by Raymond Gray.

Raymond Gray has been incarcerated since 1973. Mr. Gray has learned from life, and hard times, and even from love. His artwork reflects all of these.

BIOGRAPHIES

AUTHOR

Roger Smith holds a degree in English education and formerly taught in the Los Angeles public schools. Smith did volunteer work with youthful inmates at a juvenile detention facility in Los Angeles. He currently lives in Arizona.

SERIES CONSULTANT

Dr. Larry E. Sullivan is Associate Dean and Chief Librarian at the John Jay College of Criminal Justice and Professor of Criminal Justice in the doctoral program at the Graduate School and University Center of the City University of New York. He first became involved in the criminal justice system when he worked at the Maryland Penitentiary in Baltimore in the late 1970s. That experience prompted him to write the book *The Prison Reform Movement: Forlorn Hope* (1990; revised edition 2002). His most recent publication is the three-volume *Encyclopedia of Law Enforcement* (2005). He has served on a number of editorial boards, including the *Encyclopedia of Crime and Punishment,* and *Handbook of Transnational Crime and Justice.* At John Jay College, in addition to directing the largest and best criminal justice library in the world, he teaches graduate and doctoral level courses in criminology and corrections. John Jay is the only liberal arts college with a criminal justice focus in the United States. Internationally recognized as a leader in criminal justice education and research, John Jay is also a major training facility for local, state, and federal law enforcement personnel.